Dark Days

Jane Louise Haines

PublishNation
www.publishnation.co.uk

About the Author

I started writing poetry when I was going through a dark time in my life. At the age of 15, I started suffering with depression, an eating disorder and anxiety. Writing poems came easily and was a release, from what was going on in my head.

Dark Days is about those times when we lose hope, on our dreams and future. Life gets tougher and we have to learn how to survive, both physically and mentally.

There are many dark days in life, but there is also light at the end of the tunnel and brighter days will come.

INDEX

Dark Days

When I Was Young

When I was young I used to play
the sun used to shine every day
there was no violence, there was no crime
life was good and it was mine

When I got older we used to talk
together forever, we would walk
along the paths for miles and miles
life was good and well worthwhile

Now that I am older, I have my dreams
because I know life isn't all it seems
there are many paths that lead astray
there are many cloudy and rainy days

I aim to change the day of tomorrow
to wipe out all of my sadness and sorrow
the sun will shine again once more
but my dreams will last forever more

Death before Dawn

Gently she lay down to rest
having tried so hard to do her best
gazing up, into the evening sky
waiting for time to carry her by
Trees in the woods whisper her name
the little fawn was in so much pain
she could not answer, could not reply
but in her mind she said goodbye
She lies there alone, poor little fawn
knowing her fate, death before dawn

Illusion

Looking down into the bleak city
I close my eyes to hide the pity
The drowning noise, of traffic passing by
skyscrapers reaching up into the sky
Multi colours of graffiti on the wall
crumbling buildings, threatening to fall
Old men, lying in the street
yesterday's newspaper covering their feet
Dirty trains pass down the line
the boundary between their world and mine

Loneliness

He celebrates Christmas alone this year
but still has decorated the tree
forces a smile at the fireside
pours himself a whisky

Presents lie there unopened
wrapping paper has faded away
the old man has arranged them
shows them in display

As night draws near
the fire begins to die
he closes the curtains
slowly begins to cry

He raises his glass
this was no time to mourn
his wife would have celebrated
the day that she was born

The Flame

A lonely flame in the night
patterns playing against the light
the orange glow so comforting
a powerful image is beckoning
Beauty enhanced in the finest way
this is a candle made to portray
flickers softly one last time
this memory will always be mine

Fairy-tale

Jack and Jill have gone away
no-one knows where, no-one can say
Baa Baa Black Sheep hasn't any wool
a farmer ate him, to keep his stomach full
Little Jack Horner has no pie to eat
evicted from his home, now living on the street
Robin Red Breast flew away
the barn was vandalised where he did stay
Humpty Dumpty had a great fall
his head was smashed in, during a brawl
Three blind mice were knocked down
as they were strolling through the town
The Piped Piper still roams around
but away from reality, the other characters found

The Sacrifice

The child is dragged away from the crowd
screaming, kicking and pleading aloud
a bait for the sacrifice, Satan's surprise
his mother weeps and looks on in despise
Nothing she can do now but pray
that they will meet again someday
He holds his head up to the sky
the last tear before he dies
gently drops to the ground
the crowd goes quiet, there is no sound
The boy's cries finally cease
as his soul fights for eternal peace

Destruction

From the tip of the mountain
to the depths of the sea
from the greatest eagle
to a frantic bee
my whispers feel the bitterness in the air
as God's creations flee from despair

Across the meadow
as far as can be
into the forest, where no one can see

Run into the night
my soul is alive
away from destruction
man cannot revive

Solo

Back and forth, to and fro
the swing moves slowly in rhythmic flow
no-one rides, only the breeze
an old entertainer made to please
Dark wooden seat has rotted away
a historic reminder of child's play
it won't be here for very long
still it rocks, to its sad song

Drift on Dreams

Birds blend into the sunset across the sky
I am feeling uneasy, but don't know why
everything seems peaceful, everything seems right
colours are so warm in the evening light

As I look beyond the harbour, right out to sea
past memories are haunting and searching for me
they carry me back to many years ago
I see a small boat, rocking to and fro

Its passengers, a girl and a boy
their faces filled with happiness and joy
the waves are high, it's too dangerous to ride
suddenly the boy falls over the side

His sister panics, calls out to him
she must save him, he cannot swim
she dives down deep, into the oncoming wave
one thing on her mind, his life she must save

The boy grabs her hand, holds on very tight
so much determination and willingness to fight
she struggles to keep the two of them afloat
gradually she makes it back to the small boat

The boy pushes past and the girl moves aside
watching him reach safety, fills her heart with pride

Now she must act quickly, or meet her fate
but the stormy waters proves it's too late
they wash her away with a protesting cry
waving to the little boy, one last goodbye

Too Late

The light shines no more
sea creeps away from the shore
wind whistles, but isn't heard
feathers fall from the bird
Seeds are planted, but cannot grow
for hands are too late and cannot sew
Dreams are shattered, like panes of glass
dead flowers, dried brown grass
Take one more step, do not cry
kiss the world one last goodbye

Death Chase

The little cub was out of breath
he must keep going or meet his death
his mother urged him on to run
their game was murder and not for fun
Podgy men, the evil beast
hounds awaiting for their feast
'You must keep going', the mother did cry
'They will not stop until we die'
The mother's words flowed from the heart
which soon the hounds would rip apart
'I love you mother and always will'
'just be quiet, keep very still'
'they may not see us, may not smell'
'perhaps those creatures will return to hell'
But the hounds were near, quickening their pace
enjoying the thrill, the excitement, the chase
the vixen and her cub, now in sight
ready to taste blood and enjoy the fight
The hound's teeth sunk in deep
leaving their bodies in a small heap
Now all is silent upon the hill
nothing moves all is still
light is drained into darkness brace
until tomorrow, another death chase

Dark Rider

With the scarf wrapped tightly around her neck
she set off on her midnight trek
something had made her venture outside
she was tired and no longer wanted to hide
The police had told her, they were doing their best
'Just take it easy, get some rest'
that wasn't enough, he was still out there
he would track her down almost anywhere

She knew he was there, beyond the gate
no turning back, for it was too late.
he moved closer, eager to strike
the large black shadow on his motorbike

'What are you doing, don't do this to me'
he flashed on his main beam, she could not see
the engine roared out a rumbling cry
as if warning her, she was going to die

She stood there terrified, beginning to shake
every bone in her body about to break
The blow was hard, her heart pounded fast
there was so much pain, in that one hard blast
She lay there, waiting for the lights to fade
now the price had been paid

Electric Chair

All alone in the dark room
looking for light through the gloom
a small window reveals his doom
it will be his turn very soon
The key turns in the lock, the door opens wide
three broad officers step inside
they grab him tightly by the arm
he stands up calmly, hides his alarm
They drag him off, out of sight
from the darkness, into the light
His footsteps echo, like a lost cry
now it was his turn, his turn to die

Life

Her eyes soft and pure
more than words can say
her senses diminishing
each and every day
Knowledge comes with experience
as memory begins to block
body has no impulse
mind receives no shock
Her husband was caring
very much the same
they experienced heartache
they experienced pain
Though, they had many happy times
long, long ago
scarred upon her face
only lines do show

Nightmares

Nightmares demanding pain and sorrow

diseased world for each tomorrow

It only reflects upon me and you

what disaster can one mind do?

The Loner

His mind wandered from the road ahead
focussing his eyes on the moon instead
rounded, mystified, pale ball of night
watching over him on this bitter night
Suddenly the car jerked to a halt
an unexplained process, which was nobody's fault
The seatbelt prevented him from being harmed
even so, he was alone and alarmed
A moment that anyone would have dread
he turned the ignition, battery was dead

The route ahead seemed so far away
dark, desolate road, would lead him astray
his only chance to survive the night
would be to lock his car door, very tight

He sat their searching, listening for sound
no warnings, or threats could be found
but there was another, out there somewhere
someone who knew, that he was there

Gale force winds pounded through loose leaves
as a distant shadow approached from the trees
thunder clouds collected the flow of moonlight
sharp blood stained axe, hid from sight

His body shivered in waves of fear
as a scraping noise was heard from the rear
he turned around quickly, prepared for a shock
striking his fingers, against the door lock

There was nothing there, nothing he could see
it was just branches from a nearby tree
a muffled thump sounded from the front
as though with an instrument, rather blunt

Again, he saw nothing was there
he would not venture outside, he would not dare
the wind was blowing far too strong
he had a feeling, that something was wrong

Out the corner of his eye, a man stood to the right
hood pulled up, balaclava wrapped tight
in his hand, an axe hung low
it suddenly swung up and the car took the blow

He screamed and panicked, started pushing back
the man moved forward, there was a huge crack
windscreen shattered, glass pierced his face
blood trickled down his head, his heart began to race

The man leaned in, trying to open the door
his feet slipping, on the muddy forest floor
now was the chance, to make a dash
he darted from the car, as he heard a heavy crash

He focused on the trees, their dark leafy shape
his only chance to try and escape
almost there, just a few meters more
he felt the blow, before he heard the roar

His body landed hard, face first on the floor
raising his head, blood began to pour
his hand severed, the axe now lay
as the figure stood over him, he began to pray
The moon looked down on him, overhead
with a beaming smile ...... 'you're dead'

Close your eyes

A little boy lies awake
keeping alert, for his own sake
his father beats him, both day and night
living is just one constant fight
Wounds are hurting, through blood stained vest
body is tired, but he refuses to rest
he hears footsteps outside his door
his father has come, to hurt him some more

Mirror Image

The woman who wishes she was slim
fingers down her throat
wipes the mascara from her eyes
takes off her coat
Pins her hair back
stands up straight
smiles and is ready to go
opens the door, takes a deep breath
some things you will never know

Get Out

She lies awake, in the midnight gloom
heart beating fast, alone in the room
he will be back soon
the key in the door
soft footsteps on the stairs
making his way across the floor
The bedroom door will push wide
he will stand there and stare
she will pretend she's asleep
he will continue to glare
Eyes fixed wide, he will stand by the bed
looking down on her
thoughts pounding in his head
Those eyes will begin to see things
that aren't really there
jealous rage will begin to fire
anger begins to flare
Eruption inevitable, the devil inside
reasoning his enemy, darkness his guide
She will close her eyes tight
pray for the morning and brace for the fight
She can hear her breath.
her heart beats fast
he's here…please help!

Insomnia

Staring into the darkness
the clock ticks loud
tossing and turning
thoughts swirl in my head

Midnight crawls by
soon it will be dawn
not a wink of sleep
just a room full of thoughts

The harder I try
I tire even less
consumed with energy
the night rolls on

In the morning I will dress
put on that smile
you will never know
how I feel inside

Shadow

The black shape slinks past, into my room
curtains move in the wind
I can see him in the window, watching the moon
sitting so silent, so still
I begin to stir and gently awake
I look over to where he was sat
nothing there but memories, of Shadow
my old black and white cat

The Ugly Side of Life

The teen sat in his room
wrists scarred by a knife
hiding in a haze of smoke
The ugly side of life

Beer bottle on the side
the man who beats his wife
TV muffles most of the sounds
The ugly side of life

Standing on the bridge alone
thoughts running rife
closing his eyes as he takes a leap
The ugly side of life

Pride

He wipes the steam from the mirror
to catch a glimpse of his hair
The wig he places upon his head
wondering what he will wear
He paints his lips a crimson red
practices that smile
Colours his eyes the wildest blue
picks a dress out from the pile
Some shoes to match
the bag held tight
on the stage he will go
Not listening to the whispers in the crowd
he will give them all a show
The names they shout can hurt so much
tears him up inside
'This is who I am"
"this is my life"
I hold my head with pride

One Shot

The man who strikes a blow
at the young kid in the crowd
impressing his friends, with a girl
who's being a bit too loud

Head that touches the concrete floor
impact with a heavy blow
those twinkling eyes fading fast
blood begins to flow

You stand above, the mighty man
how strong you feel inside
his body convulses in spasms
quickly you lose your pride

Those fatal seconds, you hit him hard
down he must go
you never meant to kill him though
how were you to know

His mother will sob, tormented in pain
every night of her life, she will cry
The young lad, who spilt his drink
never should have died

Karma

This is to those, who have done some wrong
a message that you should know
The rapist, the murderer, the paedophile
and the thief who stooped so low
Karma will come and get you
even if you run
chase you into the night
hunt you with it's gun
Karma cannot be tamed
it is a wild card
It will come back to haunt you
hit you twice as hard

Paths

The paths we choose
high or low
straight, or into the night
across the clearing
around the bend
or hidden out of sight
These paths decide our future
which way is right or wrong
some routes, a short dark trek
others tiresome and long

The journey can be a hard one
depends which way we go
It can take us through the deepest valley
where the path can stoop so low

Sometimes we get lost, along the way
need help to find our way home
a friend to guide us back on track
to help us, when we are alone

The stars will shine, up in the sky
through the darkness of the night
sun will beam at your journeys end
with the brightest gleam of light

Many of us experience dark days
at some time in our life.
There is help and advice out there.
Things will get better…

Printed in Great Britain
by Amazon

66663089R00024